MONSTER TRUCKS

RYAN EARLEY

MIGHTY TRUCKS

TABLE OF CONTENTS

A Pelican Book

SEAHORSE PUBLISHING

Teaching Tips for Caregivers and Teachers:

Research shows that one of the best ways for students to learn a new topic is to read about it.

Before Reading

- Read the title and predict what the book will be about.
- Read the "Words to Know" and discuss the meaning of each word.
- Read the back cover to see what the book is about.

During Reading

- When a student gets to a word that is unknown, ask them to look at the rest of the sentence to find clues to help with the meaning of the unknown word.
- Motivate students with praise and encouragement.

After Reading

- Discuss the main idea of the book.
- Ask students to give one detail that they learned in the book.

Sight Words

a	four	is
all	go	most
are	have	the
big	in	this

Words to Know

dirt

engine

monster truck

roll cage

wheels

This is a
monster truck.

SWAMP THING
monster truck

All monster trucks are big.

DRAGON
BIGFOOT
4X4X4
30 Years
Firestone

All monster trucks have four big **wheels**.

Slingshot
wheel

roll cage
SUMMIT

Most monster trucks have a **roll cage**.

All monster trucks have a big **engine**.

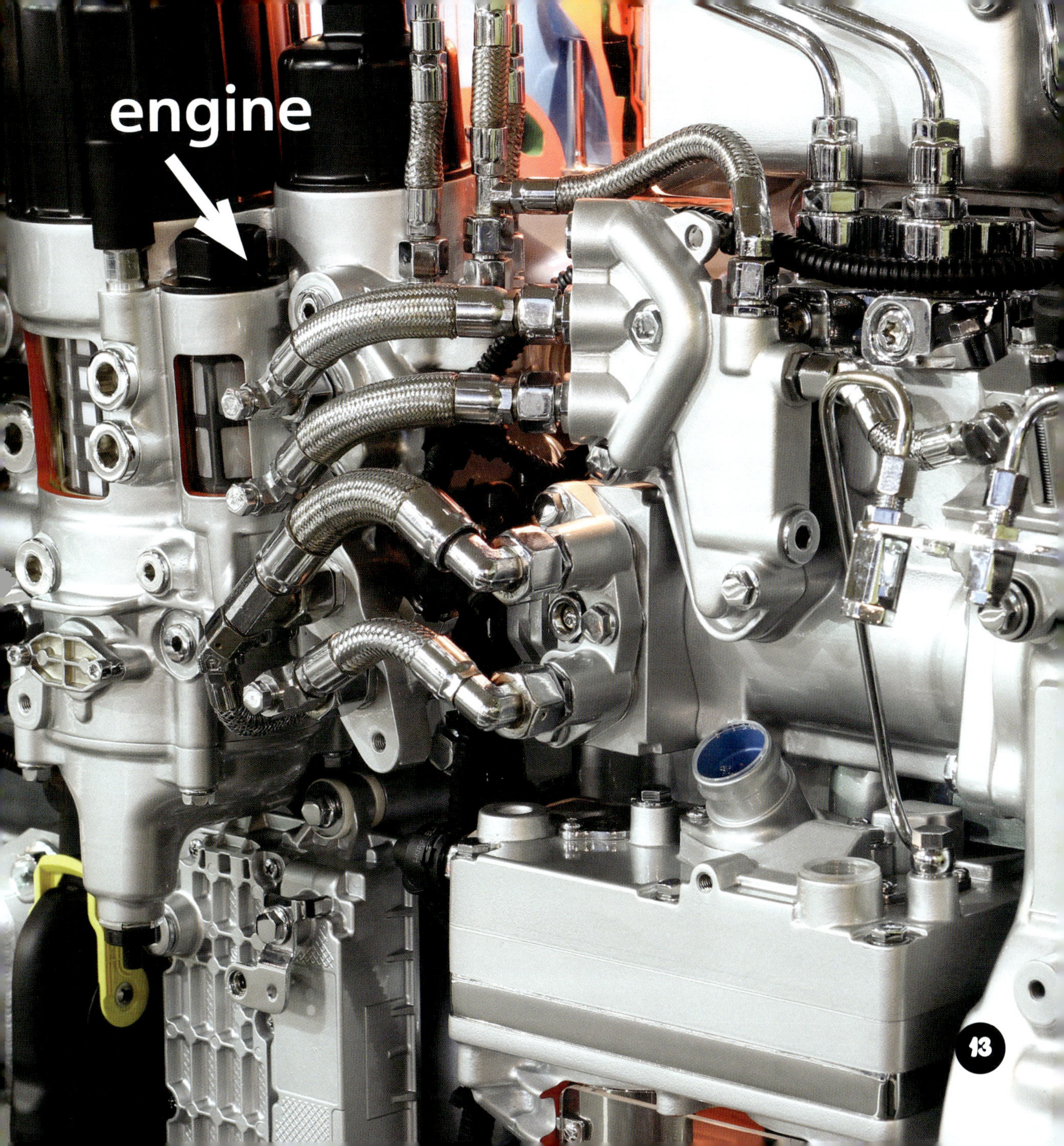
engine

Most monster trucks go in the **dirt**.

El Toro Loco
BKT
dirt

Index

Written by: Ryan Earley
Design by: Savina Magaro
Editor: Kim Thompson
Series Development: James Earley

Photos: BW Press: cover, p. 14-15; Pavel L Photo: p. 4-5; Michael Stokes: p. 7; Nigel Jarvis: p. 9; Fancy Media: p. 10-11; photostar72: p. 13

Library of Congress PCN Data
Monster Trucks / Ryan Earley
Mighty Trucks
ISBN 978-1-6389-7947-0(hard cover)
ISBN 979-8-8873-5006-6(paperback)
ISBN 979-8-8873-5065-3(EPUB)
ISBN 979-8-8873-5124-7(eBook)
Library of Congress Control Number: 2022942283
Printed in the United States of America.

Seahorse Publishing Company
seahorsepub.com 1-800-387-7650

Published in the United States
Seahorse Publishing
PO Box 771325
Coral Springs, FL 33077

SEAHORSE PUBLISHING